FRAN TARKENTON

MASTER OF THE GRIDIRON

FRAN TARKENTON

MASTER OF THE GRIDIRON

By Dorothy Childers Schmitz

Reprinted 1978, 1980

Library of Congress Catalog Card Number: 77-70890. International Standard Book Number: 0-913940-63-1

Design - Doris Woods and Randal M. Heise

When Fran Tarkenton was a little boy in Athens, Georgia, he collected bubble gum cards. His prize collection was the one of the Eagles football team. The Philadelphia team was his favorite and he adored them.

Fran not only collected the cards, he played pretend games with them. In his room, the talk would go like this: "Steve," Fran would say to the Steven Van Buren card, "We're going to run you wide a lot today." And Fran would pretend that Steve answered, "OK, Coach."

Fran would run in from school, go to his room and play these games. In the make-believe games, his team always won, of course.

But Fran also liked to play the real game. At first he was small for his age. By the time he was twelve, he was catching up. As he grew taller and stronger, he played basketball, baseball, and football.

In 1953, Fran made the high school varsity team in all three of his favorite sports. And he was only a freshman! What he liked best was baseball. He became the star pitcher for the Athens High team. Now he dreamed of being a major league pitcher.

In the 1955 season, one of the big games was with Covington. Fran stood on the pitcher's mound. He knew that he was pitching to a good hitter. So he decided to give the ball something extra. But something snapped. It was a tendon in his elbow. And it was the end of his dream of a baseball career.

Fran was disappointed. But when his arm healed, he found that even though he could no longer throw a baseball, he could still toss a football. He worked to get his arm into shape. When football season came around, he found that he could throw as high and hard as ever!

Fran played baseball, basketball, and football in high school.

Fran was a leader in high school, in clubs as well as sports.

It was his junior year. In the first game, he threw for two touchdowns. The Trojans won. They won the next one. And the next! After ten wins, it was time for the playoff. The game was with Rockmart. The Trojans had lost a close one to Rockmart the year before. This time they beat Rockmart, 26-7.

Then the Trojans were off to Valdosta for the state championship. Most people expected the big Valdosta team to win. Were they surprised! The Trojans won the state championship, 41-20.

There were two Tarkentons on the Athens High School team. Fran wears number ten. His older brother wears number twenty.

Now it did not seem to matter so much to Fran that he could not have a baseball career. When he graduated from high school in 1957, he had played such good football that many colleges wanted him. He had also been a good, all-around student. He chose the University of Georgia.

Fran was the quarterback of the freshman team. They won every game!

Fran with Coach Butts and teammates at the University of Georgia.

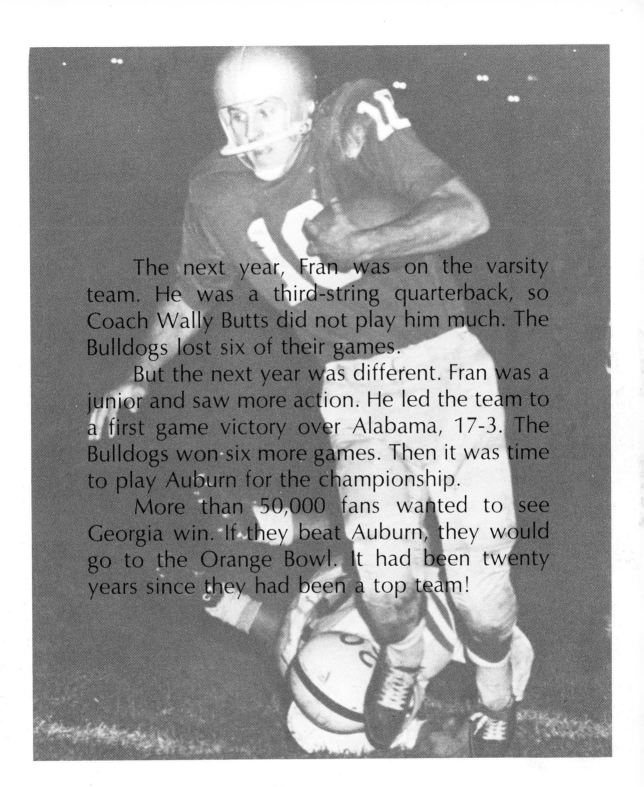

The next year, Fran was on the varsity team. He was a third-string quarterback, so Coach Wally Butts did not play him much. The Bulldogs lost six of their games.

But the next year was different. Fran was a junior and saw more action. He led the team to a first game victory over Alabama, 17-3. The Bulldogs won six more games. Then it was time to play Auburn for the championship.

More than 50,000 fans wanted to see Georgia win. If they beat Auburn, they would go to the Orange Bowl. It had been twenty years since they had been a top team!

Fran gains yardage on a missed tackle.

Fran's winning TD pass to Billy Herron in the Auburn game.

The game with Auburn was close all the way. With less than a minute left, Fran hit Billy Herron with a pass. Herron carried the ball over to tie the score, 13-13. The kick was good. Georgia won, 14-13. They were on their way to the Orange Bowl!

Georgia met Missouri in the bowl game. Fran threw two touchdown passes. Georgia won, 14-0!

The Bulldogs beat Missouri in the Orange Bowl.

The next year was Fran's last year at the University. With six wins and four losses, the team did not do as well as it had. But it was a good year for Fran himself. He made All-American and his record looked good to the pro-football scouts.

Fran and his college sweetheart, Elaine Merrell, a majorette.

Fran and Elaine with teammate on their wedding day.

At the end of that year, Elaine Merrell became Mrs. Francis Asbury Tarkenton. She had been his college sweetheart, a majorette in the Georgia band, and one of his best fans.

Now it was time for Fran to think about his pro-football career. He was drafted by the Minnesota Vikings. The Vikings were a new team then. Their coach was Norm Van Brocklin. He had been the quarterback of the team on Fran's bubblegum cards, the Philadelphia Eagles.

Fran began to work out with the Vikings. He soon learned that playing pro ball was different from playing college ball. Some of this he learned the hard way.

After the first week of training, he realized that he was in the big leagues. Working out with men who had played pro ball for ten years was a real workout! Fran said, "When you worked out with players like that, you realized how far you were from Broad and Lumpkin Streets in Athens, Georgia."

But Fran never thought of quitting. He knew he could work hard and be good enough to play with the best of them.

Fran looks over the defense.

Coach Van Brocklin called him "Peach" because he was from Georgia. Some of the players called him the "Preaching Passer" because he was the son of a minister. He had even been named after a missionary friend of the family, Francis Asbury. Fran was a good sport about it all. The rookie quarterback began to form fast friendships with other members of the team.

Fran with his Viking coach, Norm Van Brocklin.

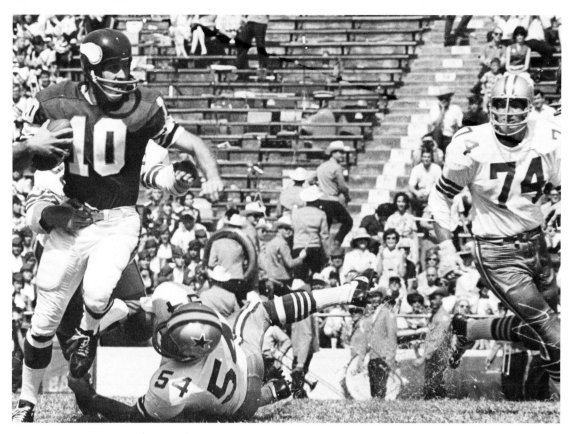

Fran shows his running style against the Cowboys.

Fran got a taste of what pro ball was like in the first game with the Chicago Bears. As a rookie, he was not the starting quarterback. But the coach sent him in. He had trained hard and studied hard. It paid off. Fran completed 17 passes for 250 yards. Four of them were touchdown passes. They beat the Bears, 37-13. People were shocked. A new team had beaten the Chicago Bears!

The Vikings were on their way. They felt confident of their new team and of their rookie quarterback. Maybe they were too confident. They lost the next game to the Dallas Cowboys, 21-7. Then they lost the next seven games.

Even though they were losing, they were learning. Fran was learning one thing that was going to make him famous. He found that when his line was not able to form a "pocket" to protect him, he could often save the play by running around until he had a chance to pass. This action would make him known as the "Scrambling Quarterback."

The next game was with the Baltimore Colts. It was close. In the last quarter, the score was 21-20 for the Vikings. Fran ran a touchdown to make it 28-20. They had won the ninth game after all those losses. They finished the 1961 season 3-10-0.

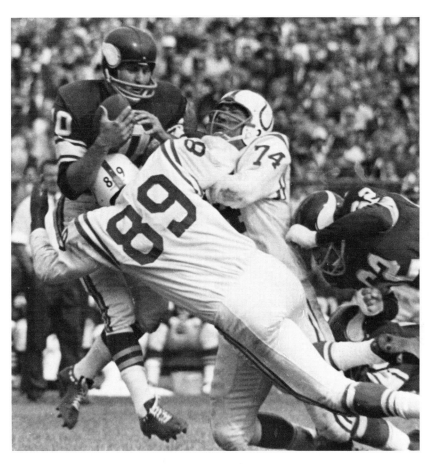

It takes two Colts to bring Fran down in this play.

The next two seasons were not much better. But the new team from Minnesota was getting what they needed most - experience. Fran was no longer a rookie. He was making a name for himself.

Fran had become a father, too. A baby girl was born to the Tarkentons in 1964.

When the 1965 and 1966 seasons did not go well, Fran thought about leaving Minnesota. He did not want to leave. But he and Coach Van Brocklin had different ideas about what would make the Vikings a championship team. It was very hard for Fran to decide. Fran said, "The Minnesota Vikings were my life, my family. It was no easy thing to decide to leave behind a bunch of guys I loved as much as I loved my own brother."

Finally he said to himself, "Francis, you can't go back there and pretend that you agree with what's being done. So you'll have to leave the Vikings. Any other decision would be unfair to the coaches, the owners, the fans, and most of all to your fellow players." So the decision was made.

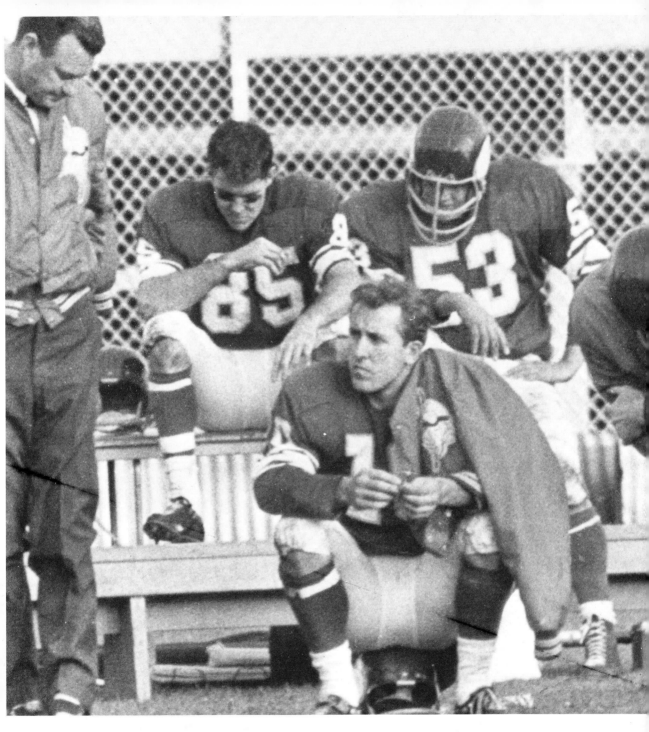

Coach Van Brocklin suffers another loss with Fran and teammates.

Fran was traded to the New York Giants in March, 1967. Coach Allie Sherman was glad to have the "Scrambler." The Giants had been in trouble in 1966. They had won only one game. The new quarterback had his work cut out for him.

The first game was with the St. Louis Cardinals. It was 10-7 for the Cardinals at halftime. But the second half belonged to Fran and the Giants. They scored four touchdowns in the second half to win 37-20!

The Giants were off to a good start. But they lost the next two games. Then it was back to New York to play with the New Orleans Saints.

The Giants took an easy lead on their home field. The New York fans wanted another win. But by the last quarter, the Saints had come back. The score was 21-20 for New Orleans. Then Fran passed for the winning touchdown. The Giants won, 27-21. The fans went wild!

Fans cheer Fran and his teammates at Yankee Stadium.

The greatest win for the Giants that season was against the Cleveland Browns. The Browns had had a great season. They started out the same way against the Giants. Then Fran and his team scored 38 points against them in the last three periods. The Giants won, 38-24!

When the season was over, the Giant's record was 7-7. Things were looking up.

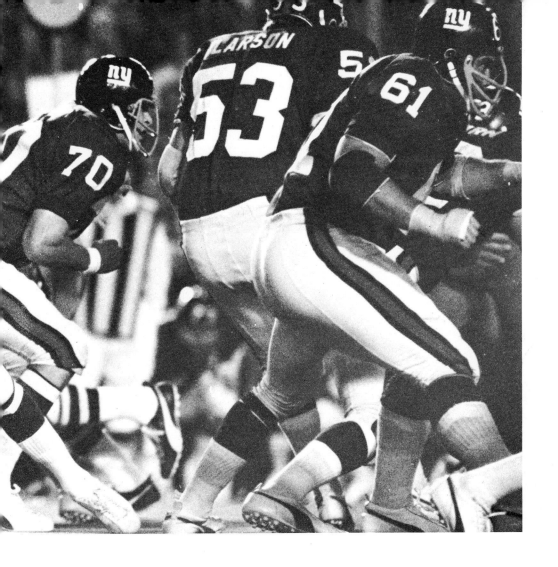

1968 began like a dream. The Giants won their first four games. It was their best beginning in 27 years! They finished the season in second place.

The 1969 season saw them finish second again. But they could not seem to reach that goal every team wants - first place.

Coach Sherman was replaced. Fran began to think about going back to Minnesota. The Vikings' new coach was Bud Grant. The Viking defense was much better now. But they needed help on offense.

By 1971, Fran Tarkenton was a name every football fan knew. The Vikings paid a big price to get him back.

Back in Minnesota, Fran praised the defensive team. He said, "I could wish for no better. Now it's up to me to produce touchdowns." And he did.

During the season, he completed passes for 2651 yards and 18 touchdowns. Fans were comparing him to Johnny Unitas. Unitas himself said, "Fran calls the right plays, moves the team down field, and gets touchdowns. That's what a quarterback is supposed to do. He gets the job done."

With Fran back, the Vikings came very close to getting to the 1972 playoffs. But they lost to the mighty Green Bay Packers, 23-10.

The 1973 season was even better. Fran led the Vikings to a 12-2-0 record for the season. In the playoff games, 27 seemed to be their magic number. They beat the Washington Redskins, 27-20. Then they took the Dallas Cowboys, 27-10!

This is what the Vikings had been working for all season. This was what Fran Tarkenton had wanted since he was their rookie quarterback! The Vikings were on their way to the Super Bowl again. The Vikings had lost the 1970 Super Bowl game while Fran was with the New York Giants.

They went against the Miami Dolphins in Rice Stadium in Houston, Texas. But the Dolphins had won the big one the year before. They wanted it again. They beat the Vikings, 24-7.

The Vikings knew they could get there again. So they looked forward to the new season. They would return to the Super Bowl.

And they did. Again they won the division title with a 10-4-0 record. When they beat the Los Angeles Rams, 14-10 in the playoffs, they were off to Super Bowl IX!

The Pittsburgh Steelers had won their bid to the Super Bowl. So it was the Vikings against the Steelers at Tulane Stadium in New Orleans. The Steelers won, 16-6. The Vikings were disappointed. Every team wants to win the big one. Fran and his teammates vowed they would get there again.

The Vikings finished the 1975 season, 12-2-0. But they lost their playoff game to the Cowboys, 17-14. After three disappointing trips to the big one, they would not be going to Super Bowl X.

Once again the Vikings looked ahead to the next season. Fran Tarkenton was not one to look back on what might have been. He looked ahead and began to plan again. He helped his teammates to do the same.

At the end of the 1975 season, he was given the Jim Thorpe Trophy as the Most Valuable Player in the NFL. It is the oldest and highest award in pro football.

Fran was never idle during the off season. He ran his business from Atlanta. He took vacations with his family. By now he and Elaine had three children. He kept in shape for football. He had a habit of throwing footballs for practice every day. He could toss one into the air and hit it with another one! When the weather was too bad to be outside, he threw footballs at a mattress in the attic! This kind of practice made him the best. It gave him that control that everyone talked about at the end of the 1975 season. Many sports writers were saying that he was better than ever in his fifteenth season of football.

Fran and the Vikings looked forward to the start of the 1976 season. What a great year to go to the Super Bowl! Fran said, "Getting through the playoffs is the hardest part." He knew what he was talking about. He had led his team through the playoffs twice before.

Vikings play in all kinds of weather.

Before the season began, everyone was talking about Fran's records. He was being compared to Johnny Unitas more and more. But Fran himself did not seem to care as much about records as his fans did. He said, "I'm much too involved in being part of the team to worry about records. Last week they said I threw my 3000 completion and I don't even remember throwing it," he laughed. "The real challenge for me is to go out there every Sunday and give a quality performance."

Maybe he was not thinking of records, but the news people were. And so were the fans. He had already passed Unitas' records' in attempts (5367), completions (3019), and touchdowns (295). He was only 100 yards away from that 40,000 yard record.

Fran passed that record in November in a game the Vikings lost, 14-13. But the team went on to beat Detroit, 31-23. Then Seattle fell to the Vikings, 27-21. They beat Green Bay, 17-10. The Vikings finished their season, 11-2-1. Finally, it was playoff time again.

It looked like 1974 again. The Vikings were playing the Rams in Bloomington for the NFC title. Early in the second half, the Vikings were leading, 17-0. Every fan was already looking to the Super Bowl. The game ended, 24-13. The Vikings were on their way to the big one again.

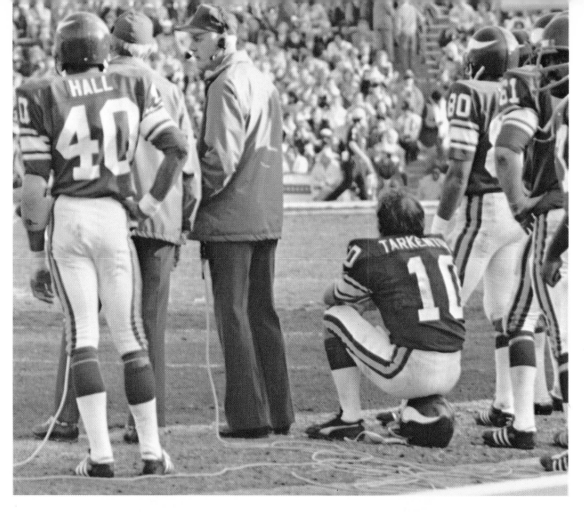

Teammates wait on the sidelines and hope.

Hopes were high. Fans expected a win this time. Fran and his teammates were hopeful. Suspense grew between the Vikings and the Oakland Raiders as game time drew near. Fran now held all the passing records. At age 36, he still showed such enthusiasm for the game and for his team. He said, "The only way we can be stopped is to stop ourselves."

It was time for all the talk to stop. It was January 9, 1977 in Pasadena, California. Super Bowl Sunday had finally come. Soon millions of fans would know if their team was the best of them all. Whether the Vikings won or the Raiders, the Super Bowl would have a new champion. Neither team had ever won before. The Vikings really wanted to win Super Bowl XI. But it was not to be. The Raiders won, 32-14.

Fran and all the Vikings were stunned. They had gone to the big one again. But for the fourth time they were going home without the victory. The Vikings gave the Raiders the credit they deserved. They had played a better game.

Someone had asked Fran how he would like to be remembered. He said, "I'd like to be thought of as a good quarterback. I hate to think I won't be unless I win a Super Bowl."

His coach had something to say about that. Coach Grant said, "I don't think there is any question that Francis is going to go down as the greatest quarterback ever to play the game, period. But his greatest attribute is his enthusiasm for every part of the game. He is a doer, not a doubter."

Fran and coach Grant look worried.

The 1977 season was a tough one. The Vikings weren't winning as easily as they usually did. To make matters worse, Fran broke his leg about half way through the season. He was finished for the year, and the Vikings didn't make it to the Super Bowl.

1978 was the best year Fran ever had! He completed 345 passes, gained 3,468 yards, and made twenty-five touchdown passes. However, it wasn't good enough. Again, the Vikings didn't get to the Super Bowl.

After thinking about it for a long time, Fran decided he would quit playing. He wanted to go out on top.

When he retired on May 8, 1979, he held NFL records for most passes attempted (6,467), most passes completed (3,686), most yards passing (47,003), and most touchdown passes (342).

Coach Grant was right. Francis Asbury Tarkenton will probably be remembered as "the greatest quarterback ever to play the game."